praying
the LORD'S
prayer

How to ... Study series

Series Editor:
TERRY VIRGO

praying
the LORD'S
prayer

TERRY
VIRGO

WORD BOOKS

NELSON WORD LTD
Milton Keynes, England
WORD AUSTRALIA
Kilsyth, Victoria, Australia
WORD COMMUNICATIONS LTD
Vancouver, B.C., Canada
STRUIK CHRISTIAN BOOKS (PTY) LTD
Cape Town, South Africa
CHRISTIAN MARKETING NEW ZEALAND LTD
Havelock North, New Zealand
JENSCO LTD
Hong Kong
JOINT DISTRIBUTORS SINGAPORE –
ALBY COMMERCIAL ENTERPRISES PTE LTD
and
CAMPUS CRUSADE, ASIA LTD
SALVATION BOOK CENTRE
Malaysia

PRAYING THE LORD'S PRAYER

© Frontier Publishing International Ltd. 1987, 1993

ISBN 0-85009-627-8 (Australia 1-86258-299-6)

Unless otherwise indicated, Scripture quotations are from the New International Version (NIV), © 1973, 1978, 1984 by International Bible Society.

Created, designed and typeset by Frontier Publishing International, BN43 6RE, England. Reproduced, printed and bound in Great Britain for Nelson Word Ltd. by Cox and Wyman Ltd., Reading.

93 94 95 96 / 10 9 8 7 6 5 4 3 2 1

THANK YOU TO ...

I am very grateful to Mary Austin for all her hard work in listening to recordings of my preaching on this theme and for working through my notes in order to present this book to you in its present form.

Also available in the *How To* series:

FOREWORD

The *How To* series has been published with a definite purpose in view. It provides a set of workbooks suitable either for housegroups or individuals who want to study a particular Bible theme in a practical way. The goal is not simply to look up verses and fill up pages of a notebook, but to fill in gaps in our lives and so increase our fruitfulness and our knowledge of God.

Both of Peter's letters were written to 'stimulate ... wholesome thinking' (2 Peter 3:1). He required his readers to think as well as read! We hope the training manual approach of this book will have the same effect. Stop, think, apply and act are key words.

If you are using the book on your own, we suggest you work through the chapters systematically, Bible and notebook at your side and pen in hand. If you are doing it as a group activity, it is probably best to do all the initial reading and task work before the group sessions — this gives more time for discussion on key issues which may be raised.

Unless otherwise stated, all quotations from the Bible are from the New International Version.

Terry Virgo
Series Editor

Contents

INTRODUCTION

From my early days as a Christian I was greatly influenced by a godly pastor who emphasised the importance of prayer, not only through his preaching but by his own lifestyle.

I followed his example and tried to become a man of prayer. Over the years many have influenced me by their lives, teaching and books. I found I was often very stimulated to pray by reading the stories of great praying heroes of the past, but these books rarely told me how such men actually expressed themselves when they knelt before God. What did they actually say to the Lord day by day? How did they arrange their priorities in prayer?

When we are in a crisis we find prayer comes naturally! Maintaining a steadfast prayer life day by day presents a different kind of challenge! How often have you resolved to pray more? Perhaps you have tried to make a fresh start only to be disappointed and disillusioned and even condemned. Instinctively you know you must not give up but often you wonder how to succeed in the disciplines of regular prayer.

It is my conviction that the Lord's Prayer is a wonderful provision from God to help us in our problem. Several years ago my own prayer life was wonderfully helped by seeing the Lord's Prayer as God's answer to my dilemma. For years now I have built my own devotional life on this structure, so this book is something of a personal testimony. I strongly recommend that you consider building your daily prayer life on the structure of the Lord's Prayer. This book is particularly designed to be a practical guide to you as you follow that course of action.

From time to time I have found myself preaching on this subject and, more recently, have found that the Holy Spirit is impressing upon me in a new way how important it is. I am praying that every person who seriously works through this book will find their prayer life dramatically changed to the glory of God and the advance of His Kingdom.

Terry Virgo

Chapter One

LORD, TEACH US TO PRAY

Christ's soldiers fight best on their knees.
D.L. Moody

No man is greater than his prayer life.
L. Ravenhill

I have resolved to devote an hour each morning,
noon and evening to prayer — no pretence, no
excuse whatsoever.
John Wesley

Throughout the ages those we view as the 'great saints' have all proclaimed prayer to be the secret behind their powerful ministries. These 'ordinary Christians' simply took to heart the teaching of the Bible which exhorts Jesus' disciples to 'pray and not give up' (Luke 18:1), be 'faithful in prayer' (Rom. 12:12), 'keep on praying' (Eph. 6:18), 'devote yourselves to prayer' (Col. 4:2) and 'pray continually' (1 Thess. 5:17), and they got results.

However much we may envy their success, the fact remains that prayer is as available to us as it was to them. The same God who proved Himself strong for them is willing to be sought by our generation. Prayer is one of the most vital issues facing Christians today. We live in a demanding age. The very speed of life and the pressures of the modern world conspire to overwhelm our spiritual walk. God is looking for individuals who, through prayer, are keen to allow the power of the Spirit to be manifest through them to the world at large. But how do we pray?

Jesus' disciples instinctively knew that they needed to be taught how to pray. They therefore came to Him and simply asked Him to teach them. We too must realise that there is a way to pray effectively — a learning process which all of us need to discover for ourselves. We may have tried before to establish a prayer pattern, but with limited success. Though our flesh is weak, we must never forget that our spirits are willing!

The apostle Paul in no way condemns us for our weakness. Instead, he acknowledges it, stating that 'we do not know how to pray' (Rom. 8:26 RSV), but adding that the Spirit is there to help us. Without the Spirit's touch, the Lord's Prayer is a mere ritual. But when the Spirit brings its importance to our hearts, it becomes the most dynamic prayer that we can ever offer to the Father.

THE TEACHER

The 'great prayer warriors' of the past and, for that matter, the present, could teach us much about prayer. Imagine being an apprentice alongside Elijah, Wesley or Paul Y Cho! How much we should learn! And yet, when it comes to teaching the subject, none of these men knows better how to instruct us in prayer than our Lord Jesus Christ. There are several reasons for this.

HIS POSITION

The Son was perfectly united with His Father in every way. Jesus said:

> I and the Father are one (John 10:30).

Jesus was intimately in touch with the Father. He knew God's character so He was fully aware of how the Father would act in different circumstances. He knew the extent of God's power and how He wanted to manifest it. He knew God's will and how He planned to accomplish it. There is no better teacher than one who knows his subject so perfectly.

HIS PRACTICE

Prayer played a vitally important part in Jesus' life. We read:

> Very early in the morning, while it was still dark,
> Jesus got up, left the house and went off to a
> solitary place, where he prayed (Mark 1:35).

The day before this time of prayer, Jesus had preached in the synagogue, driven out an evil spirit there, released Simon's mother-in-law from a fever and been host to the 'whole town' who had gathered at the door for teaching, healing or deliverance (Mark 1:21–34). We might have expected Him to 'have a lie in' and 'recover quietly'. Instead, He minimised His rest time because of the greater need He had to pray.

Jesus' life was packed with activity. God had 'anointed [Him] with the Holy Spirit and power' and was 'with him' (Acts 10:38) in all He did. He triumphed as a man, yet He never worked independently of the Father. He openly declared:

> the Son can do nothing by himself; he can do
> only what he sees his Father doing, because
> whatever the Father does the Son also does
> (John 5:19).

If Jesus had not kept in touch with God through prayer, He would have been acting on His own initiative. But this was not God's way. He wanted to tell His Son what to do and because of this, Jesus placed top priority on His secret relationship with Him.

> After leaving them, he went up on a mountainside
> to pray (Mark 6:46)

> Jesus went out to a mountainside to pray, and
> spent the night praying to God (Luke 6:12).

Jesus knew that it was only when He had received from His Father that He could pass anything on to the people. The best teacher not only knows his subject, he has had personal experience of it.

HIS PRAYER

Jesus prayed that we might enjoy the same unity with the Father as He had with Him.

> My prayer is not for them alone. I pray also for those who will believe in me through their message, that all of them may be one, Father, just as you are in me and I am in you. May they also be in us so that the world may believe that you have sent me (John 17:20,21).

This oneness is maintained by prayer. Jesus longs for His pupils to take note of what He says and to act on it.

THE TEACHING

PROVISION

We might have expected Jesus to respond to the disciples' request by emphasising the importance of inner attitudes to prayer or the help of the Holy Spirit. Instead, He provided them with a prayer framework just 57 Greek words in length which we have come to know as 'the Lord's Prayer'.

One of the purposes of this book is to rediscover the mighty power of this 'God given' tool. Most of us learnt the Lord's Prayer as children. It was destroyed for us in school assemblies where we chanted it mindlessly. As a result, we tend to see it sometimes as 'a prayer for the children' or 'the family prayer'. I want to remind you that it was originally uttered by Jesus in reply to a request for instruction about prayer by His front-line troops.

Battle-hardened apostles who had seen the amazing impact of Jesus' ministry and knew about His prayer life asked Him earnestly to teach them to pray. He answered them by giving this formula.

Jesus said that the Father was not impressed by 'vain repetitions' (Matt. 6:7 AV) so it was never His intention to present to us a prayer that we should learn to recite like parrots. The outline He gave us was meant to consist of a number of headings on which we build our prayers. God knows how prone our minds are to going off at tangents when we pray. If we want to establish sustained, disciplined and regular prayer, we need help. Jesus offers us that help by providing us with the answer — not a 'principle of prayer' nor an 'endless list of things we've got to pray about' but a structure — a structure that most of us probably know by heart.

> Without fervour form becomes formality.
> Without form fervour becomes fever.

PRIORITY

When many people come to God in prayer they adopt their own prayer formula. This often involves beginning with confession of sin in order to 'clear the way' to God. Initially, this might seem wise but in reality it can result in a systematic digging of a large hole of self-condemnation. By the end of the exercise the individual concerned lies in a bedraggled, whimpering heap about two metres below ground level!

The danger of making confession of sin our priority is that we run the risk of becoming preoccupied with self at a time when we should be focusing on God. We naturally need to pray for forgiveness but it is not the best way to begin. How readily Satan takes the opportunity of greeting us at the door of prayer and diverting us into a total side-track!

Maybe it's never really occurred to us that Jesus' formula for prayer must be the best. There is ample evidence from Scripture that when we follow Him we receive His blessing. It was when the

servants at the wedding at Cana did what Jesus told them that a
potentially embarrassing situation was averted (John 2:1–11). It
was when the blind man obeyed Jesus by going to the pool of
Siloam to wash that he came back seeing (John 9:1–7). It was when
Peter responded to Jesus' call that he was able to walk on the water
(Matt. 14:29). It is impossible to improve on Jesus' prayer structure. It must take priority simply because it's the best one.

PRACTICE

Some people argue that they don't need to focus much on private
prayer because they pray while they walk the dog or drive the car.
Whereas continual prayer is encouraged by Scripture, we also
need to recall that Jesus told us to:

> go into your room, close the door and pray to
> your Father who is unseen (Matt. 6:6).

Jesus had continual fellowship with God yet it was still His
practice to spend time alone with Him as well. Finding a place
away from everyone else may prove to be a problem for us — but
not an impossibility or Jesus would never have asked us to do it.
It may have escaped our attention that He grew up in a poor home
with brothers and sisters who would have made demands on His
time. He probably didn't have His own room either. And when
Jesus actually began His ministry no one could have been busier,
yet He fiercely guarded His prayer life and frequently escaped
from people to a quiet place where He could talk to His Father.

> crowds of people came ... But Jesus often
> withdrew to lonely places and prayed (Luke
> 5:15,16).

Personal prayer is a great power which is most effective when
practised in the best way possible. A garden fork can be used as
a rake but it's far more efficient when used to turn over soil.

Similarly, unstructured prayers can and do work, but their effectiveness is infinitely increased when we take Jesus at His word and pray like this:

> Our Father in heaven,
> hallowed be your name,
> your kingdom come,
> your will be done on earth as it is in heaven.
> Give us today our daily bread.
> Forgive us our debts, as we also have forgiven
> our debtors.
> And lead us not into temptation, but deliver us
> from the evil one
> (For yours is the kingdom and the power and the
> glory for ever. Amen.)
> (Matt. 6:9–13).

Consider your own experience of prayer.

Pray earnestly that God will speak to you as you read this book and that He will transform your prayer life.

Chapter	Two

OUR FATHER IN HEAVEN

The Jews of Jesus' time had a very exalted view of God and established hundreds of laws which had to be obeyed to satisfy Him. He was the great Jehovah who had performed many miracles for His people. He stood alone, almost unreachable, above His creation. Bearing this in mind, can you imagine the look of astonishment and shock on His disciples' faces when Jesus told them to begin their prayers: 'Our Father in heaven'?

'Religious' people today also seem to have a very lofty view of God and often establish laws about how to reach and satisfy Him. Some feel that chanting will work them into God's presence; others prostrate themselves before crosses or idols; many repeat legalistically various prayer forms and some actually inflict physical pain on themselves as penance for their wrongs. Even Christians can consciously or unconsciously keep God at a respectable distance. Maybe they, like these 'religious' people, have been so preoccupied with honouring and serving Him that it's hard for them to stop and see Him as 'Father'.

The apostle Paul told the Galatian Christians, 'You are all sons of God through faith in Christ Jesus' (Gal. 3:26). And Jesus Himself said to His disciples, 'the Father himself loves you because you have loved me and have believed that I came from God' (John 16:27). If you are a Christian, you are a member of God's family and are dearly loved by Him.

OUR FATHERS ON EARTH

For some of us, praying to God as Father poses something of a problem. This is because we tend to base our idea of what a heavenly Father is like on what we have experienced of our earthly fathers. We effectively transfer their way of relating (or not relating) to us onto God and assume that He will treat us in the same way. It stands to reason, then, that if we have a negative attitude towards our earthly fathers, we'll withdraw from someone who wants to be called 'Father'. After all, who wants to pray to a person he doesn't actually want to know?

Whether we're aware of it or not, we may find ourselves 'playing safe' with God by being content to appreciate with our heads alone that He loves us. We somehow avoid experiencing that love in a deeper way. Before we can relate effectively to God as Father, we need to be released from any negative attitudes towards fatherhood that our own fathers may, even unknowingly, have caused us to adopt.

Do you find it relatively easy to relate closely to God as Father?

Where do you find most difficulty in your relationship with God? (e.g. I see Him as a rather judgemental person; He seems very distant from me; I find it hard to trust Him for financial provision; He frightens me; I tend to feel that He doesn't understand, etc.)

Now consider your relationship with your earthly father and identify where the difficulties may have come from.

Over the next week or so, pray (with others, maybe) that God will release you from these areas of difficulty and reveal and deal with any others which may still be hidden from you.

SONS 'IN LAW'

What made Jesus' earthly relationship with His Father so good was that it was based on love. At His baptism, God declared:

> You are my Son, whom I love; with you I am well pleased (Luke 3:22).

From the very start, Jesus relaxed in His sonship and allowed His ministry to flow from the knowledge that He was loved and totally accepted by His Father. We must have the same attitude. God knows that if we drift from His love, we will become fearful, anxious and act independently of Him. That's why His Word exhorts us, 'Keep yourselves in God's love' (Jude v.21). There are two main ways in which we can do this:

RUNNING AWAY — EXCITEDLY

The world often seems to offer far more attractive alternatives to the disciplined (boring?) Christian life and we can easily become convinced that Jesus was actually the one who came to steal, kill and destroy. The devil seems to offer a far more abundant life! If you've run away like this, you will probably find yourself thinking like the younger son in Luke 15. He believed he had ruined his rights to sonship. Although he was coming home with the word 'father' on his lips, he actually expected to be received as a mere household slave.

> Father, I have sinned against heaven and against you. I am no longer worthy to be called your son; make me like one of your hired men (Luke 15:18,19).

But when he arrived back home he discovered, to his astonishment, that his father refused to receive him back as the servant he thought he deserved to be.

But the father said to his servants, 'Quick! Bring the best robe and put it on him. Put a ring on his finger and sandals on his feet. Bring the fattened calf and kill it. Let's have a feast and celebrate' (Luke 15:22,23).

So if you've been running away from God, remember that when you return to Him He will not 'beat you' as a master might discipline his disobedient, wayward slave. The idea of receiving you back as a servant will never enter His mind. Instead He will welcome you home as His son or daughter and rejoice over you.

STAYING AT HOME — MISERABLY

The elder brother in this parable seemed to take the more commendable step by staying at home. His decision to do this, was absolutely right but his attitude towards being there was hopelessly wrong. When his younger brother returned, he commented to his father:

> Look! All these years I've been slaving for you and never disobeyed your orders. Yet you never gave me even a young goat so I could celebrate with my friends (Luke 15:29).

This is the response of a servant, not a son. He didn't realise it, but he actually treated his father as 'master' and had never enjoyed a loving relationship with him. His preoccupation had always been with service. To him, his work rate was the all-important means by which to measure devotion. It's no wonder, then, that he was so indignant with his father when his younger brother 'who has squandered your property with prostitutes' (Luke 15:30) came home to such jubilation.

Some of us are more concerned about being God's servants than the Father's sons or daughters. We do all the 'right things': read the Bible, say our prayers, go to church and offer a hand to the needy, but all of them are done in a dutiful way — because they're expected of us as Christians. And, if we're honest, we can't stand it when some backslider returns from a life of utter godlessness to the most glorious of celebrations!

Read Galatians 5:1.

Consider what God wants for you. What mustn't you allow to happen to you? How do you do this?

SONS 'IN LOVE'

Perhaps the highlight of the Luke 15 parable is that the father went out to both his sons and invited them to forget past waywardness and legalistic attitudes and to celebrate his love again. Maybe we, like them, need to respond.

If God loved me and send His Son to die for me while I was still a sinner (Rom. 5:8), then He loves and accepts me whether or not I prayed today, or yesterday, or if I haven't got down to it for weeks. This is because Jesus satisfied God on my behalf by keeping His Father's requirements.

I can relax in God's grace and love. I'm not required to prove my worth to Him. Jesus is my righteousness so I don't have to manufacture it, I can't earn it, I don't deserve it, but I'm in it! I stand complete in Christ. I have died to the law (Rom. 7:1–6) and am under no condemnation whatsoever (Rom. 8:1,2). It's simply impossible to get God to love me any more or any less than He does now. His love for me is already complete because it's exactly the same love that He has for His Son, Jesus.

God sees each Christian as a vital part of His family and He longs to be known as 'Father' by everyone, not just a chosen few.

I will be a Father to you, and you will be my sons and daughters, says the Lord Almighty (2 Cor. 6:18).

He doesn't only want to be known as someone who expressed His love by sending Jesus to die for us. He wants us to experience the outworking of His love on a practical day to day basis as well.

> **If God is for us, who can be against us? He who did not spare his own Son, but gave him up for us all — how will he not also, along with him, graciously give us all things? (Rom. 8:31,32)**

God is worth spending time with. If we knew a human being like Him we'd want to be in that person's presence all the time! Jesus, who radiated the Father's life, drew crowds to Himself. People never felt that they *had* to be there, they *wanted* to be. He accepted them as they were and they talked to Him freely and naturally about anything that concerned them.

How much easier it is for us when we are sons who want to pray than slaves who feel we've got to! Legalism falls away at this point and discipline takes over. The difference between the two is that legalism comes from an effort to obey external laws in order to justify and prove ourselves to God, to others and even to ourselves. Discipline is motivated by the Spirit from within and brings us into freedom.

Yes, we do need discipline in prayer and that will require working at, but we need never fall back into slavery and legalism again. Someone once said, 'The Lord doesn't want an efficient, gleaming machine, He wants a loving heart.' Jesus never taught us to pray 'Our Master in heaven' so when we come to Him, let's always tune into God's Fatherhood and rejoice as His sons and daughters in the security of His love.

A legalistic Christian might declare:

> **How adequate is the affection the Almighty Lord has offered us, that we should be called slaves of the Most High!**

What's the Bible version? (1 John 3:1)

To pray: Our Father in Heaven

Forget the problems which are concerning you at the moment. Relax with God — as His child. Talk to Him freely and naturally about things He has done for you recently, and thank Him for them.

Chapter Three

HALLOWED BE YOUR NAME

Although we enter into prayer as sons talking to our Father, there is another equally important side to our relationship with Him that we dare not forget. Jesus made reference to it when He prayed 'Holy Father' (John 17:11). In doing this He brought together beautifully the intimacy and awesomeness of God.

For us to have a sound understanding of who He is, we need to hold both these truths. God is not just Father, neither is He only majestic Lord. If we over-emphasise His Fatherhood we will tend to drag Him down to our level; if we over-concentrate on His holiness we will not be able to lift ourselves up to His. The secret lies in grasping both aspects of God's character and balancing them so that neither outweighs the other.

In the last chapter we spoke of God's Fatherhood so now let's turn to consider His awesomeness. In Deuteronomy 10:17 the Lord is described as:

> God of gods
> Lord of lords
> the great God
> mighty and awesome
> who shows no partiality
> and accepts no bribes

Various individuals who encountered this holy God would never forget the experience.

Consider what happened to Ezekiel, Daniel and John
in Ezekiel 1:28; Daniel 10:8 and Revelation 1:17.

What do you think it was that caused them to react in
these ways?

BE JOYFUL!

Praising God in song is an important part of hallowing His name.
David declared:

> I will extol the LORD at all times; his praise will
> always be on my lips (Ps. 34:1).

It is clear that David had determined in his heart that he would
worship God even when the world around him was falling apart at
the seams. Habakkuk too resolved that no matter what disasters
came his way he would rejoice (Hab. 3:17,18). The positive
attitudes of these men were adopted by many individuals in the
Old and New Testaments and the exhortation to 'rejoice in the Lord
always' (Phil. 4:4) extends to us too.

Sometimes, we shall sing to God with genuine enthusiasm. On
other occasions, 'declaring His majesty' will be about the last thing
we shall want to do! God understands our feelings and we need to
remember that whatever happens to us He is still the Lord in
control of everything. And He is still worthy of our praise. Our faith
in Him is displayed as we look up hymns which particularly glorify
Him and lift our voices in adoration regardless of our circumstances.

> Immortal, invisible, God only wise.
> In light inaccessible, hid from our eyes.
> Most blessed, most glorious, the Ancient of
> Days.
> Almighty, victorious, thy great name we praise.

Consider the sort of people who are exhorted to rejoice in Psalm 34:2.

Why do you think that believers are encouraged to rejoice in adversity?

Pray that God will give you the grace to rejoice whatever your circumstances.

It is important to remember that our priority in prayer is not to present to God a number of personal needs but to glorify Him. If we make a habit of doing this, we shall be delivered from self and sin-centredness. If we then run out of time, it's far better that we have placed the greater emphasis on praising Him than on asking Him for things for ourselves.

GOD'S NAME

Jesus taught us to pray that God's name would be hallowed. To 'hallow' means to reverence, sanctify or keep holy. The Jews of the Old Testament were so conscious of the holiness of God that they would not even say His name. Instead, to avoid the term 'Jehovah', they actually referred to God as 'the Name'.

Names in the Bible were important because they said something about a person's character. God even changed some names because the new ones He chose for people were more appropriate to them. If names therefore inform us of people's characters, the 'Name' tells us what is true about God. But although people's names can be altered, God is unchanging. He says of Himself: 'I AM WHO I AM' (Exod. 3:14).

There are actually many different aspects of God's character which are contained in His name. It's rather like looking at a beautiful diamond whose many facets each contribute to the magnificence of the whole. Each facet is a part of the diamond yet, at the same time, is separate in identity.

Some of the different names which reveal the person of God to us are:

Jehovah Jireh	the Lord will provide
Jehovah Rapha	the Lord that heals
Jehovah Nissi	the Lord our banner
Jehovah Shalom	the Lord our peace
Jehovah Ra-ah	the Lord our shepherd
Jehovah Tsiadkeni	the Lord our righteousness
Jehovah Shammah	the Lord is present

How would we know that God provides for us unless He told us? Why would we go to Him for peace if we didn't know He could offer it? The good news is that He has told us about Himself and His name stands for everything that He is.

David declares, 'Praise the LORD, O my soul; all my inmost being, praise his holy name' (Ps. 103:1) and goes on to acknowledge the graciousness of God throughout the Psalm. If you know God's name you will trust in Him (Psalm 9:10).

LORD, WE LIFT UP YOUR NAME

It's one thing for us as individuals to experience the awesomeness of God but Jesus had more than a 'personal awareness' in mind when He encouraged us to pray to God 'Hallowed be your name'.

Let's look back at the Old Testament for a minute. In Exodus chapters 7–14 we read of the astounding miracles that God performed for the Israelites against the Egyptians. When the Israelites experienced first hand the power of God which destroyed their enemies they reacted in two ways.

the people feared the LORD and put their trust in him and in Moses his servant (Exod. 14:31).

It's apparent from these reactions that they came to experience the wonder of God's name for themselves. In a song of praise for their deliverance they declared: 'The nations will hear and tremble' (Exod. 15:14) which is exactly what happened. When two spies were sent to Jericho before the Israelites captured the city, they were informed by one of its inhabitants:

> a great fear of you has fallen on us, so that all who live in this country are melting in fear because of you. We have heard how the LORD dried up the water of the Red Sea for you ... When we heard of it, our hearts sank and everyone's courage failed because of you, for the LORD your God is God in heaven above and on the earth below (Joshua 2:9–11).

God's name was lifted up, it was glorified, it was hallowed. The same fear of God fell upon all who heard what happened to Ananias and Sapphira when they lied to the Spirit and died for it.

> the whole church was appalled — great awe and strange terror and dread seized them — and all others who heard of these things (Acts 5:11 Amp).

What actually happened was that Peter spoke God's 'holy' name into the situation that faced him and God responded by revealing Himself as 'holy'.

We too can do this by taking one of God's names (either one mentioned in this chapter or another from Scripture) and by praying it into situations.

For example, let's take the name 'Shepherd'. God, our Shepherd, leads us and looks after us. Ask the Holy Spirit to remind you of people you know who are searching for God's guidance at this time. Are you aware of any who are upset and need the tender care of a Shepherd God? Pray His name into these situations asking that He will be glorified as 'Shepherd'. Tomorrow you can choose another name (Rock, Helper, Gardener, Deliverer, Strength ...).

Your prayers need never become repetitive if you adopt this method.

WANTED — FAITHFULNESS

God's promise to the Israelites was that if they listened to and followed Him, He would not only bless them but cause Himself to be feared by His enemies.

> If my people would but listen to me,
> if Israel would follow my ways,
> how quickly would I subdue their enemies
> and turn my hand against their foes!
> Those who hate the LORD would cringe before him,
> and their punishment would last for ever.
> But you would be fed with the finest of wheat;
> with honey from the rock I would satisfy you
> (Ps. 81:13–16).

The Israelites, however, refused to listen to and submit to the Lord.

Read Ezekiel 36:16–38.

Note how the Israelites defiled the land, what God decided to do with them and what God said about His name.

Although it is true that God will vindicate His great name among the nations in spite of us, He longs to do this through us. Today the way we as Christians conduct our lives will either honour or dishonour God among those who do not know Him.

Read Romans 2:17–24 and consider whether you are dishonouring God in any area of your life (e.g. bearing grudges, gossiping, associating with the wrong sort of company, etc.).

Ask God to show you how you could honour Him more (e.g. by offering hospitality, giving away money, serving in the Sunday School, etc.).

Jesus' one consuming passion was that His Father's name be glorified. The way He lived reflected this and so did the way He sought to bring God's authority into situations He faced. Let's put behind us our failure to represent God's majesty to a world which lies in darkness and ignorance of His true nature. And let's learn how to pray His name into different circumstances as His Spirit directs.

> Great is the LORD in Zion; he is exalted over all the nations. Let them praise your great and awesome name — he is holy (Ps. 99:2,3).

To pray: Hallowed be Your Name

Choose a hymn or worship song and sing it to the Lord. Ask God to bring to your mind one of His names.

Pause to allow Him to remind you of people/countries/circumstances, etc. into which He would like you to pray this name. Pray, trusting God to honour His name in each situation.

Chapter Four

YOUR KINGDOM COME

INVASION

Have you ever thought that Christians are actually living on enemy-occupied territory? 'The whole world is under the control of the evil one' (1 John 5:19) and this kingdom of darkness corrupts everything around us — education, governments ... When Jesus came to earth He arrived as an invader on a rebel planet and met the selfishness, hypocrisy and sickness of man head on. He came as a 'warrior king' intent on conquest and His aim was more than the offer of salvation.

The reason the Son of God appeared was to destroy the devil's work (1 John 3:8).

In other words, He came to release the world from Satan's grasp by bringing a new Kingdom to earth — the Kingdom of God.

'Your kingdom come' (Matt. 6:10) is the battle cry Christians take from Jesus and present to the world. To pray this prayer we need to have a true understanding of the nature of the Kingdom. Clearly we've got to know what to expect if we're asking it to come!

OFF-COURSE

There are several theories about what the Kingdom of God is. Some of these are totally wrong while others contain valuable Kingdom principles but all short of a complete understanding of what the Kingdom represents. Let's look at some of them.

THE KINGDOM IS:

The general evolution of good over evil

In the 19th century there was a belief that as time passed things would naturally get better. All we needed was improved housing, education, health-care and so on. What some called 'evolutionary improvement' others interpreted as the 'advancement of the Kingdom'. The trouble was that as we entered the 20th century the world was not seen to be 'on the up'. Rather, with the passing of two world wars and with the steady increase in crime, it had to be noted that man was slipping further into the quicksand rather than working his way out of it. In reality his refusal to honour his Creator (Rom. 1:18–32) led him into darkness and was the cause of his decline — not his improvement.

Simply another word for the church

The church is the 'bride of Christ', the company of people who have been 'called out'. The Kingdom is far broader in scope than the church. The relationship between the two is that the church is the agent which brings in the Kingdom.

The fact that God is king over everything

We cannot dispute the fact that God is king over all nations and history but this is not to be understood as the Kingdom of God. This is because Jesus spoke of the Kingdom drawing near and advancing.

Simply having Jesus in your heart

While we would wholeheartedly agree that everyone needs to have a personal experience of salvation, it's not sufficient to view the Kingdom as something purely individual. It's actually far more dynamic than that.

Gained through secular battles for social justice (liberation theology)

In some countries, there are individuals who 'take the sword' and strive to break through the repressive measures meted out by those in authority. They seek to build an army of 'freedom fighters' in the name of 'liberation theology' — fighters who will bring in what some of them understand as the 'Kingdom of God'. But Jesus said, 'My kingdom is not of this world. If it were, my servants would fight' (John 18:36).

Although the liberation theologians are misguided in their interpretation of the Kingdom of God, they do quite rightly emphasise that the Kingdom has much to say to social needs. Jesus came preaching good news to the poor (Luke 7:22) and wherever the gospel has broken through in power there have been amazing social changes.

Past revivals have seen women and children treated better, health standards, working hours and conditions improved and help offered to the elderly. The Kingdom is more than just having church services. It speaks to the needs of society. The nations must begin to feel the impact of a church which is getting on its feet and bringing in this sort of change.

A future era

Some people believe that we are currently living in a gospel era and that there is a Kingdom era still to come. This idea actually has its roots in the Old Testament where the prophets pointed ahead with great expectancy to what they called the 'day of the Lord'. They looked forward to a future age when the valleys would be raised up and the mountains brought low (Isa. 40:4). This 'terrible' or 'glorious' day would be ushered in by the Messiah and once He had come the new age would begin.

PRAYING THE LORD'S PRAYER

We are not actually waiting for a Kingdom age to come. We are, in fact, in it now! When Jesus, the Messiah, came He brought in a new government on His shoulders (Isa. 9:6). When we repented and believed the gospel, we stepped into that government or Kingdom and began tasting the 'powers of the coming age' (Heb. 6:5). We passed from death to life (1 John 3:14) and became new creations (2 Cor. 5:17). We now have the privilege of experiencing eternal life (John 3:36) and are able to enjoy the power of the Spirit which God promised to pour out in the last days (Joel 2:28).

Jesus said:

> if I drive out demons by the finger of God, then
> the kingdom of God has come to you (Luke
> 11:20).

The manifestation of the power of God demonstrates to all that the Kingdom, though not fully come, is now among us.

MANIFESTO

A 'manifesto' is a declaration of policy or intentions issued by a sovereign or commander. God's manifesto was in the form of a promise to His Son.

Note this promise in Psalm 2:6–8.

At the last supper, Jesus told His disciples that the Father had appointed a Kingdom for Him but made it clear that He was allowing them to share it too (Luke 22:29).

Consider the following verses: Daniel 7:13–14,18, 22,27.

Although much of the interpretation of Daniel's dream awaits a future fulfilment, it has present day significance. God wants us to reign with Christ. He tells us he's pleased to 'give [us] the kingdom' (Luke 12:32) and the implication is that He will give it now Christ is our head and we, the church, represent His body (Col. 1:18). If we're part of Him then what happens to Him must also happen to us. The great purpose of history is fulfilled as Christ establishes the Kingdom through His people.

We have the tremendous privilege not just of possessing an entrance ticket to the Kingdom of God but of ruling with Jesus in it! When we pray for the Kingdom to come we are asking for God's promise to His Son to be fulfilled — namely that the nations and the ends of the earth will come into His possession. We are praying too that the rule of Christ shall be manifest in the world through signs and wonders, the release of captives and the forgiveness of sinners who devote themselves to their new King.

WARFARE

Jesus' ministry began with a declaration of war on the earth. His mission was to prove Himself stronger than Satan by binding him (Luke 11:21,22) and releasing the prisoners under His control (Luke 4:18). He shared the mission with the seventy-two who, like Him, went out and performed miracles. They returned with great joy that even demons submitted to them in Jesus' name. He replied:

> I saw Satan fall like lightning from heaven (Luke 10:18).

The idea that the church is a 'cosy club' is foreign to New Testament teaching. The world is a battleground; Jesus is our commanding officer and every Christian is a soldier who needs to arise, dump his cup and saucer in the church kitchen and put his armour on! There is simply no time to waste.

Read Luke 9:57–62.

What sort of things can hinder our progress with God?

The mission is ours, it's urgent and we need to be involved in it. The Kingdom advances forcefully but it's only forceful men and women who lay hold of it (Matt. 11:12). We need to take the warfare seriously by maintaining an ever-increasing passion for the advancement of the Kingdom on earth.

This means that firstly that we've got to be ruthless with personal faults and wrong doing by being prepared to:

> throw off everything that hinders and the sin that
> so easily entangles (Heb. 12:1b).

The Kingdom makes great demands of us. We can't afford to tolerate weaknesses or play with sin. And we must not only want to overcome them, they must actually be dealt with. The 'Kingdom character' is shown to us in the Sermon on the Mount (Matt. chapters 5—7) and we need to pray for that quality of life to be present in our churches today.

Secondly that we must pray not simply for the advancement of an 'internal kingdom' within each believer. We must go beyond that and ask God for a visible manifestation of His presence and power among His people.

The healing of the sick and the casting out of demons, the recovery of the deaf, dumb and blind, and the forgiveness of sinners were all works of the Kingdom. They weren't an addition to the message but a part of it. The miracles were evidence of the Kingdom of God in action.

It's all very well *telling* people about the power of God, they want to *see* it! And we need to be prepared to be the instruments through whom He reveals Himself in miraculous ways (Mark 16:17,18).

TRIUMPH

We're encouraged in the Scriptures to 'look forward to the day of God and speed its coming' (2 Pet. 3:12). When we can see the goal ahead, we're spurred on to reach it — in much the same way as

Christ was prepared to suffer because He saw the 'joy set before him' (Heb. 12:2). We have yet to see the day when the Kingdom will be fully established on the earth. The Bible concludes 'Come, Lord Jesus' (Rev. 22:20) and it triggers a response in our hearts: 'Amen. Come, Lord Jesus — in the future, yes, but now too — in my life, in the lives of those who do not know you, in power through signs and wonders, your Kingdom come!'

To pray: Your Kingdom Come

Ask God to advance His Kingdom in: (choose from the following)

Jerusalem: your family situation
home — you and your family
church — holiness, power, evangelism, etc.

Judea: your involvement situation — school, college, workplace, club, neighbourhood, etc.

Samaria: a known situation — friends needing help/ power, etc. A young people's conference, etc.

The ends of the earth: a world situation[1] — a particular country/somewhere where there's been a catastrophe.

---

[1]Purchase the book *Operation World* by Patrick Johnstone (STL) so that you can pray intelligently for countries you know nothing about.

Chapter Five

YOUR WILL BE DONE ON EARTH AS IT IS IN HEAVEN

The Bible doesn't tell us too much about how the will of God is being done in heaven. It does, however, reveal a great deal about someone who came from there and who obviously fulfilled His Father's will here on earth. Let's see how Jesus reacted to His task and gain some insights on how we too should react.

GOD'S WILL — OUR LIFE PRINCIPLE

Jesus' one great 'life principle' was not to satisfy His own desires but to carry out those of God. Hebrews 10:7 records the words He spoke to His Father:

> I have come to do your will, O God

and John 6:38 records the words He spoke to men:

> I have come ... not to do my will but to do the will of him who sent me.

Jesus said that doing the will of God was His 'food' (John 4:34). It was everything He lived for and all that really satisfied Him. Through childhood, baptism, temptation, conflict with sin, with sickness, and with demon-possession, through desertion and crucifixion, the driving force of Jesus' life was God's will. And at the end of His earthly ministry He could confidently declare to His Father:

> I have brought you glory on earth by completing
> the work you gave me to do (John 17:4).

How do I glorify God? Not by pleasing myself, nor by attempting what He wants others to accomplish but by fulfilling His plan for me. That's the only truly satisfying way to live.

GOD'S WILL — OUR GREAT PLEASURE

Not only was God's will Jesus' life principle, it was also His great joy to do. The Amplified Version of the Bible translates John 4:34:

> My food [nourishment] is to do the will [pleas-
> ure] of him who sent me.

God's will was not a burden to His Son, it was His delight, His nourishment and refreshment. It gave Him that feeling of fulfilment and contentment when He had accomplished it — in much the same way as we feel completely satisfied after eating a splendid meal.

God wants you to grasp the truth that His will for you will never be a burden. He knows that your hunger isn't satisfied by second-rate food and He wouldn't dream of setting before you a meal which didn't both satisfy and please you. God knows the plans He has for you and what He gives you to do will neither be too much nor too little for you to manage. It will, instead, be 'your food' and when you've found out what it is you can resolve to enjoy doing it!

> Consider whether you can declare Psalm 40:8 to the
> Lord.

GOD'S WILL — OUR EARNEST PURSUIT

How did Jesus find out what God's will for Him was? Before appointing the Twelve He spent the night praying to His Father (Luke 6:12) and we read that in spite of the demands of the crowds

He 'often withdrew to lonely places and prayed' (Luke 5:16). Wherever Jesus went He found time to stop and ask God what He should do.

In a busy world where we all want 'instant everything' it's hard to put a foot on the brake, turn off the road and consult God about whether or not we're actually travelling in the right direction! We think we haven't got time to stop when, in actual fact, we haven't got time to be in a hurry! As someone once said, 'The big trouble with communication today is the short supply of those willing to be communicated with!'

There's no need to race round like a mad thing hoping that what you're doing fits into God's plan for your life! That's silly, and the Scriptures encourage us not to 'be foolish but understand what the Lord's will is' (Eph. 5:17). If God's plan were not available to us, Paul would never have said these words, nor would He have prayed that the Colossians be filled with the 'knowledge of his will' (Col. 1:9). David was one who recognised that God's will was available to him, an individual, because he exhorted the Lord:

> Show me your ways (I want to see)
> Teach me your paths (I want to hear)
> Guide me in your truth (I want to know)
> (Ps. 25:4,5).

Are you seeking a new job? Is a relationship or situation causing you concern? Do you need somewhere else to live? Are financial problems weighing you down? What matters to you matters to God. Regardless of how big or small the issues are, God wants to be involved in them. Wait on Him. Seek Him for His will to be done in your circumstances and then do whatever He says.

Consider the areas where you need God's input in your life and pray for His will to be done in each of them. In most cases this will involve more than just one prayer so keep at it and trust God for the outcome.

GOD'S WILL — OUR DEEPEST PEACE

It's apparent that although He entered into many fierce conflicts with men during His lifetime, Jesus possessed an amazing calmness. The reason for this is that He was always aware that His life was in His Father's hands and trusted that His Father knew what was best for Him. It meant that He experienced not only the thrill of seeing people healed and set free, but also felt acutely what it was like to suffer and die. His absolute faith in God's will for His life brought Jesus a deep sense of peace.

Whereas Jesus was always confident that God's will was best, many of us are not always so sure. His faith and willingness to surrender all are often in sharp contrast to our fear and desire to hold onto everything. Surely this is because we suspect that God is really not on our side at all. We feel that He can only truly be interested in spiritual things like holiness and that if we open up completely He will only ask us to do the things we hate. Isaiah 55:8 (which was actually addressed to a rebellious nation) seems to lend weight to our argument:

> my thoughts are not your thoughts, neither are
> your ways my ways.

We conclude from this that if we want to do a particular thing the idea definitely cannot be from God. He only wants to kill our enjoyment of life and make us miserable. But God has no wish to lead a lot of Christians into doing things they don't want to do in places they don't like! He has no desire whatsoever to see us gritting our teeth and ploughing drearily on towards a place in heaven where we shall collapse in an exhausted heap! What advertisement is this to the liberating and joyful gospel of God? No, we are told that God works in us to:

> will and to act according to his good purpose
> (Phil. 2:13).

He graciously works on our wills so that they come into line with His will. When this happens we find that we actually have the mind of Christ about a certain course of action. The Psalmist declares:

> Delight yourself in the LORD and he will give you the desires of your heart (Ps. 37:4).

When God's children delight in Him, their desires become one with His and they actually find themselves wanting to do what He wants — and enjoying it too. The desire to embrace the Father's will involves absolute surrender. It means telling God that He knows best how to run your life. It means joyfully presenting your body to Him as a living sacrifice (Rom. 12:1) and discovering for yourself that His will is 'good, pleasing and perfect' (Rom. 12:2).

It's only when you release yourself completely into God's hands and begin allowing Him to have His way in your life that you will experience the deep peace that Jesus Himself enjoyed while He was on earth. The Kingdom is expressed in power when each of us chooses to know and do the will of God. Our prayer life should include a definite submission of our wills. This is the proof of true worship.

> Love, so amazing, so divine, demands my soul, my life, my all.

Consider any area(s) in your life where you suspect that you're resisting God's will (e.g. withholding tithes, need for baptism, income tax irregularities, relationship difficulties, etc.).

Commit the area(s) to Him and do as He asks you.

To pray: Your Will be done on Earth as it is in Heaven

Take time to reflect on and pray about the overall direction of your life. Pinpoint and pray through various issues in which you are seeking God's will to be done.

Pray that God will reveal any areas where you are resisting His will. Act on what He says.

Chapter Six

GIVE US TODAY OUR DAILY BREAD

GOD, THE GIVER

The sudden and dramatic change in emphasis in this prayer — from great spiritual vision to apparently mundane thoughts about daily bread — is startling. It simply serves to remind us that God cares not only about us as spiritual people, but as those who have physical needs as well. Our heavenly Father is not in the business of extracting from us everything we've got to give and then throwing us on the scrap heap like a worn out car. He made us and, like any good earthly father, He wants to look after us too.

Jesus Himself knew what it was like to be hungry, thirsty and tired and He gladly received food, drink and hospitality from people. His obvious concern for the physical needs of individuals is reflected in the way He acted towards them. When the disciples were ready to dismiss the 5,000+ people, they were amazed to find that Jesus actually wanted to feed them! (Matt. 14:15,16)

Maybe they, like many of us, thought that Jesus would only be interested in teaching spiritual things and that once He had done that, everyone was free to leave. But this was not the case at all. Similarly, on the occasion when Jesus met the disciples on the seashore after His resurrection, He invited them to enjoy breakfast before they discussed spiritual matters (John 21:10–12).

Read Matthew 15:29–38.

Meditate on verse 32 and try to understand how Jesus felt about the people. Pray that God will give you a deeper compassion for others.

THE WAY HE GIVES

GOD GIVES WILLINGLY

'God is Love' (1 John 4:8) and love, by definition, cannot withhold or remain neutral. It has to give. It is therefore impossible for God to be 'Love' and stingy at one and the same time. When we understand this, we are forced to put aside all our fears about His being a mean master. We replace these false notions with the truth that it is rooted in the Father's character to give.

> If you, then, though you are evil, know how to give good gifts to your children, how much more will your Father in heaven give good gifts to those who ask him! (Matt. 7:11)

Notice that God's gifts are not only good but that they come to those who ask Him for them. Now we might expect God to give only to those who deserve to receive but He doesn't think like that. Rather, because it's His nature to give, His blessing falls upon good and evil people alike.

> He causes his sun to rise on the evil and the good, and sends rain on the righteous and the unrighteous (Matt. 5:45).

> he is kind to the ungrateful and wicked (Luke 6:35).

Let's remember that it was while we were still sinners that Christ died for us (Rom. 5:8). He didn't wait for us to improve before He was willing to consider us as 'saveable material'. Naturally we are not to test God's goodness by living selfishly (Rom. 6:1) but we can marvel that when we let Him down from time to time He still wants to hear our requests and give to us.

GOD GIVES JOYFULLY

If 'God loves a cheerful giver' (2 Cor. 9:7), it stands to reason that it is no hardship for Him to give. He doesn't, as we sometimes do, offer things in a dutiful sort of way — 'I suppose he'd better have that!' When the lost son returned home, his father didn't look up from the table, grunt, 'Oh, so you're back!' and insist that he wash off the smell of pig before he found some old clothes somewhere and ate. No, he ran to his son, embraced him, called for the best robe, put a ring on his finger and sandals on his feet. Then he had the fattened calf prepared and held an extravagant party which included both music and dancing (Luke 15:22–25). That's God's attitude towards giving! He loves it!

GOD GIVES GENEROUSLY

Reflected in the story above is not only God's enthusiasm over giving but His extreme generosity as well. The idea that God gives grudgingly is nowhere found in Scripture. God didn't present Adam and Eve with a small cabbage patch in a corner of the Garden of Eden in which to plant a few vegetables! He gave them the whole world to rule over and enjoy! Similarly, He wasn't content just to offer His Son's ability to us, He actually allowed Jesus to die to bring us back to Himself.

Think about it. If God's highest gift is His Son, what's His most basic gift? Couldn't it be 'our daily bread'? The two are extremes. Surely God is telling us that if He's willing to give us both the most precious and the most common things, He is more than willing to supply us with everything in between. The Bible doesn't say, 'God adequately provides us with enough for our needs.' It says:

> [He] richly provides us with everything for our enjoyment (1 Tim. 6:17).

Psalm 84:11 declares: 'no good thing does he withhold from those whose walk is blameless'. When it comes to giving, God has a hard time restraining Himself! He isn't prepared simply to offer us salvation, rather, He wants us to have abundant life with abundant provision from Him (John 10:10). He has the ability to do for us 'immeasurably more than all we ask or imagine' (Eph. 3:20). The Father longs for us all to receive from Him not the blessings of a 'corner cabbage patch' but our full inheritance as sons of His.

> And God is able to make all grace abound to you, so that in all things at all times, having all that you need, you will abound in every good work (2 Cor. 9:8).

What He Gives — Daily Bread

The only time the Greek word *epiousios* (translated 'daily') occurs in the New Testament is in the Lord's Prayer. Because we have no other context with which to compare its use, there is some debate about what the word actually means.

There are three main views: bread for today, bread for tomorrow and bread from tomorrow's Kingdom (i.e. we are asking God to allow us to taste the powers of the age to come).

There is probably a very strong link between the request for daily bread in the New Testament and the provision of manna in the Old. Each morning the Israelites went out and collected enough manna for that day. Whether they gathered a lot or a little, each individual found that he always had as much as he needed (Exod. 16:18). God wanted His people to know that His grace would be sufficient for the day and that He would provide on a daily basis. Those who tried to store up manna (other than on the day before the Sabbath) found that the food went bad overnight.

Although it is not wrong to save up for things we believe God wants us to have (car, house, clothes), it is wrong to hoard. Jesus teaches us to depend daily upon God because He knows how prone we are to getting ourselves comfortable and living independently of Him. The man who decided to rely upon the crops he had stored up in his barns came to ruin (Luke 12:16–21) and James exhorts us not to boast and brag about our plans without considering what part God has to play in them (James 4:13–17).

> Consider Paul's teaching in 1 Timothy 6:17–19 bearing in mind that if you live in the West, you should consider yourself 'rich'.

> Let God speak to you through these verses.

Proverbs 30:8,9 says:

> give me neither poverty nor riches, but give me only my daily bread. Otherwise, I may have too much and disown you and say, 'Who is the LORD?' Or I may become poor and steal, and so dishonour the name of my God.

A rich man can become independent by relying on his riches. A poor man can become dependent by relying on other people's generosity. The best way, as Solomon so wisely puts it, is to pray for what we need. Our daily dependence must be on God and He tells us that He knows what our needs are (Matt. 6:32). He also urges us:

> do not worry about tomorrow, for tomorrow will worry about itself. Each day has enough trouble of its own (Matt. 6:34).

The 'bread' we are asking for includes all our material needs. It also includes the need for spiritual provision — Jesus is the bread of life (John 6:35). So we need His grace for today's demands and His ability to help anyone who may call on us. The passage about the friend at midnight follows on immediately after the Lord's Prayer and concludes with the encouragement to ask God for the Holy Spirit (Luke 11:13). The man who called on his friend at midnight based his request for bread on his relationship with him and on the fact that he knew his friend had what he wanted. His boldness in asking came out of friendship and a real desire to receive what he lacked.

Let's continue to be 'rooted and built up' in Christ (Col. 2:7) and to remember that He has the answers to all our needs. And let's persist in bringing our requests to God. Delays, disappointments and apparent refusals may come to test our faith, but we need not allow any of them to prevent us from receiving what God wants us to have — our daily bread.

Read Luke 18:1.

Consider what God wants you to do, what He doesn't want you to do and whether you are responding appropriately to this exhortation.

To pray: Give us Today our Daily Bread

Put aside any false beliefs that God does not want to give good things to you.

Ask Him to provide for your physical needs (food, health, warmth, strength, finance), emotional needs (peace of mind, joy, security in God's love) and spiritual needs (closer walk with God, greater sensitivity to the Spirit, help in counselling).

Chapter Seven

FORGIVE US OUR DEBTS AS WE ALSO HAVE FORGIVEN OUR DEBTORS

OUR NEED OF FORGIVENESS

For as long as we need daily bread, we shall need forgiveness. Although it is not a wise idea to begin our prayers by focusing on our sinfulness, we dare not completely avoid acknowledging our faults. Jesus now makes provision for us to come before the Father to seek cleansing for anything we may have done or not done which has displeased Him.

Before we need forgiveness we have to know if we have sinned. We are told in Scripture that:

> No-one who is born of God will continue to sin (1 John 3:9).

> If we claim to be without sin, we deceive ourselves (1 John 1:8).

As Christians, we are slaves of righteousness and new creations in Christ. It is therefore unnecessary for us to sin. However, all of us know that we fail the Lord at times. On these occasions we need to act on the encouragement to 'confess our sins' (1 John 1:9) and confessing our sins may seem straightforward enough on the surface but in practice, owning up to being wrong is a difficult and sometimes painful operation. It cuts across our pride to admit our faults. If we're honest, we would prefer simply to forget or justify them, major on our good points and hope that God will be satisfied. Sadly, we often really do 'deceive ourselves' and we offer all sorts of excellent reasons for our sinful behaviour. We're almost out of the habit of examining ourselves. Self-justification has become an automatic response to conviction of sin.

How do Christians excuse themselves for their faults? Some become almost sentimental about them, saying things like: 'It's my little weakness' or 'He knows I don't really mean it.' Others try to laugh off their wrongs by almost boasting about them: 'I never was the type to keep within the speed limit.' Others attempt to shift the blame elsewhere: 'Yes, I got angry with him but he deserved it.' Others feel so negative about themselves anyway that the mere hint of criticism causes them untold distress. They 'curl up' and bury their heads in invisible pillows in the hope of smothering the notion that they might have acted sinfully. They will come out only when time has robbed the initial challenge of its cutting edge.

What sort of excuses have you used in the past to justify your sin? Consider what excuses might you be using today.

When we get into the habit of justifying ourselves, we begin to lose the knowledge of what sin really is. We then adopt man-made standards of righteousness and live according to them. Then, when we do actually sin, we simply excuse ourselves and rely upon all the positive things we do to see us through. The Pharisee who went into the temple to pray was like this. He was so confident of his own devotion compared with that of others that he didn't actually need mercy from the Lord at all (Luke 18:9–12). Who needs forgiveness from God when he's already forgiven himself?

Meditate on and memorise 1 Samuel 16:7b.

Read Proverbs 21:2.

Let God weigh your heart, listen to what He says and respond to it.

THE ALTERNATIVE TO FORGIVENESS

Paul declared, 'If we judged ourselves rightly, we should not be judged' (1 Cor. 11:31 NASB). If we examine ourselves by God's standards, confess our sins and receive His forgiveness, we shall not need to be judged by Him as disobedient children who are always seeking to escape conviction of sin. If, on the other hand, we persist in avoiding acknowledgement of our wrongs, we can expect to receive judgement from God.

Ananias and Sapphira were given the chance to own up to their sin but they refused to do so and were killed (Acts 5:1–11). Similarly, many of the Corinthian believers became sick and even died because they would not examine themselves honestly (1 Cor. 11:27–30). These are extreme cases but they act as a sobering reminder that if we continue to sow to please our flesh, we shall reap destruction from it (Gal. 6:8). Judgement is God's only alternative to forgiveness.

The judgement of God comes to us first in the form of discipline, which the writer to the Hebrews encourages us to see as something positive:

> My son, do not make light of the Lord's discipline, and do not lose heart when he rebukes you, because the Lord disciplines those he loves, and he punishes everyone he accepts as a son (Heb. 12:5,6).

Discipline comes from a God who loves us too much to abandon us as we wallow miserably in our unforgiven sins. His rebuke is designed solely to benefit us (Heb. 12:10). We can choose either to rebel against Him or to 'submit to the Father of our spirits and live' (Heb. 12:9). So when He sees something about us that He doesn't like, He will tug at it gently to start with. If we release it to Him, we will know His forgiveness and peace. But if we tug it back or refuse to acknowledge that it offends Him, we will experience an increasing inner turmoil until we do actually let it go.

There were occasions in David's life when he resisted God's discipline and suffered for it. He tells us how his rebellion affected him:

> When I kept silent, my bones wasted away through my groaning all day long. For day and night your hand was heavy upon me; my strength was sapped as in the heat of summer (Ps. 32:3,4).

Holding onto his sin left him physically, emotionally and spiritually drained. He exhausted himself by being unwilling to acknowledge his faults to the Lord.

Consider an occasion when you refused to confess a sin to God. How did you feel? What was the result?

JUDGING OURSELVES WRONGLY

When we come to the point of wanting to 'judge ourselves rightly' we must beware of opening ourselves up to the devil's condemnation. He is correctly named the 'accuser of our brothers' (Rev. 12:10) for his goal is to cause us to deplore ourselves for our weaknesses and to give up on ourselves as hopeless cripples who will never be good enough for God.

Above all else, the devil seeks to make the whole process of self-examination something thoroughly heavy and negative — because he fears what blessing will come to the children of God if they really do get serious about living holy lives.

Let's remember that there is a significant difference between the devil's condemnation and the Father's conviction. The devil tends to 'wrap us up' in our sinfulness. He paints a thoroughly black picture of how much we're failing God, although he usually doesn't specify areas in which we're actually at fault. Instead, he offloads onto us a very general 'burden' of sin which is hard to deal with because it has no apparent root. When you don't know what you're meant to be confessing, how do you confess? The negative feelings about self just seem to hang around and drown us in worthlessness.

By comparison, the conviction brought by the Spirit slices into our consciences like a 'double-edged sword' (Heb. 4:12). When Nathan rebuked David, the king was not vaguely challenged about some uncertain wrong he had committed! He was struck to the core by a burning conviction of sin (2 Sam. 12:7–13). This is how it should affect us. We should learn how to reject any black cloud of condemnation that floats in our direction. God's 'lightning' comes with precision to judge 'the thoughts and attitudes of the heart' (Heb. 4:12). We should not be in too much doubt about where we have offended the Father.

Consider the ways in which the devil tries to condemn you (e.g. by telling you that you're worthless; by reminding you of 'what happened before'; by explaining what you 'ought to have done,' etc.).

Pray that God will give you grace not to listen to him. What could you do to counter the enemy's arguments?

JUDGING OURSELVES RIGHTLY

The Psalmist said:

> I have hidden your word in my heart that I might not sin against you (Ps. 119:11).

God's Word was his safeguard against sin and he carefully weighed everything he did against what the Word said. As Christians, we shouldn't have to think twice about whether or not we ought to do certain things. If the Word is in our heart we will not break our promises or cheat or lie to justify ourselves. Instinctively we should recognise that all these things are forbidden by God in Scripture.

'Judging ourselves rightly' not only means examining our conduct against Scripture, it also involves our assessing more objectively our relationships with others. Such questions as: 'Would I have been happy if he had said/done to me what I said/did to him?' should cause us to become more aware of personal failure.

Our consciences too need to be alerted — perhaps to things that we aren't doing as well as to those we are. We can become sinful by being lazy about helping others, or about writing to praise or criticise television programmes, newspaper or magazine articles. The voice of the Church needs to be heard. We are Christ's ambassadors and God is relying on us to let His thoughts be known to the world in which we live.

Ask God to highlight anything about your life that displeases Him.

THE ASSURANCE OF FORGIVENESS

When Christians begin to 'judge themselves rightly' and confess their sins, God is there to forgive them. Indeed, Jesus would never have encouraged us to pray 'forgive our debts' if He had known that the Father never actually intended to forgive us. We can have complete assurance that 'if we confess our sins, he is faithful and just and will forgive us our sins' (1 John 1:9).

Read again Psalm 32:3,4 and continue reading through verse 5.

Consider what David did and didn't do. What was God's immediate response?

Sin isn't worth holding on to! The guilt it creates in us eats away at our lives and slowly causes us to become indifferent or hard and bitter. Jesus offers us the opportunity now to search our hearts and simply to ask God to reveal what may be wrong in us. When we confess, He will forgive, and the effect of that forgiveness will often be felt in the form of release and great joy.

> WHAT HAPPINESS FOR those whose guilt has been forgiven! What joys when sins are covered over! What relief for those who have confessed their sins and God has cleared their record (Psalm 32:1,2 LB).

Forgiveness changes people. It turns hardened sinners into children of God and revolutionises the lives of those believers who daily continue to heed and respond to God's challenges.

Confess and repent of any sin that is standing between you and God.

THE RESPONSE TO FORGIVENESS

There are two elements to forgiveness — receiving it and giving it. They go hand in hand because Jesus taught us to pray 'forgive us ... as we also forgive'. Augustine referred to this request as 'the terrible petition'. We are asking God to deal with us in the same way as we deal with others. The prayer forces us to examine our attitudes to those around us. The measure of forgiveness we offer to them will determine how much forgiveness we should expect from God.

It's often hard to forgive — especially when others have badly hurt or let us down. We somehow feel justified in being angry with them and holding against them the suffering they've caused us. We want to 'get even' and sometimes actively seek to drag the other person's character down whenever we can. If we're honest, we don't really want to hear the words: 'Forgive as the Lord forgave you' (Col. 3:13). In some strange way, we almost want to bear the grudge which we often interpret as something else — 'a difference of opinion', 'a personality clash' or something similar.

It's only when we consider the debt we owe to Christ that we shall fully appreciate why we must forgive. This debt can be seen clearly in the parable of the servant who owed his master over a million pounds. Overwhelmed by the amount and in obvious distress the man fell on his knees and begged his master for time to repay the money.

Read the parable in Matthew 18:23–35.

Consider the three things that the master did in verse 27.

When we beg for mercy from God, He doesn't ponder our case for hours and work out how much He's going to lose if He forgives us. He doesn't seek to 'get even' with us when we offend Him or gloat over us while He allows us to suffer a bit longer for our failures. Instead He looks with compassion on us, immediately releases us from the whole debt and gives us total freedom from it. There are no half measures. When God gives, He gives completely. Scripture doesn't say that God forgave us most of our sins, but all of them (Col. 2:13). It also tells us that He separates us from our sins 'as far as the east is from the west' (Ps. 103:12).

When we've been forgiven like this, how can we refuse to forgive our brothers and sisters? Such statements as, 'I can't forgive him for what he's done to me', 'What she did is unforgivable' or 'I'll forgive but I'll never forget' should be foreign to us. They don't fit Bible language any more than Chinese characters fit an English dictionary. The language of the Bible is love and love freely forgives sinners.

When we withhold forgiveness, we become like the forgiven servant in the parable. He tried to deny forgiveness to a fellow servant who owed him a few pounds. For a little while, it seems, he got away with it but he was later found out by his master and punished for his lack of mercy.

We read that God is 'slow to anger, abounding in love and faithfulness' (Ps. 86:15). He is gracious to give us time to consider our ways — in this case, whether or not to forgive. If we refuse to release anyone from the prison of our resentment, our unforgiveness will actually imprison us. Whether we're conscious of it or not, we shall remain bound by our grudge for as long as we cling to it. This will have a direct and serious effect on our relationship with God, as Jesus points out.

> For if you forgive men when they sin against you, your heavenly Father will also forgive you. But if you do not forgive men their sins, your Father will not forgive your sins (Matt. 6:14,15).

Christians may feel themselves totally at a loss when faced with a demon to cast out or a man to raise from the dead! But there is no excuse for them not to be good at forgiving. Indeed, they should excel at it! When we pray this part of the Lord's Prayer, we are accepting its terms. We are saying to God that we're happy to work to the standard He has set — that in the same measure as we offer forgiveness to others, He will return forgiveness to us.

Do you agree to that?

To pray: Forgive us our Debts as we also have Forgiven our Debtors

Ask the Holy Spirit to reveal to you anything about you which may have offended the Father.

Ask God to forgive you and receive that forgiveness.

Ask the Holy Spirit to reveal to you if you are holding anything against any brother or sister. Forgive anyone who comes to mind. If necessary, put right by action the wrong you have committed — today.

Chapter Eight

AND LEAD US NOT INTO TEMPTATION BUT DELIVER US FROM THE EVIL ONE

There has been much debate about whether God actually leads people into temptation. The Bible makes it clear that God does not tempt us and that we must take personal responsibility if we fall into sin. James tells us:

> God cannot be tempted by evil, nor does he tempt anyone (James 1:13).

and he goes on to state that:

> each one is tempted when, by his own evil desire, he is dragged away and enticed (James 1:14).

But that doesn't mean that we simply wait for temptation to come and then cry out to God in a panic about it. Jesus encourages us to be alert to the approach of temptation and evil before they descend upon us. So we pray in advance that the Father will shield and deliver us from missing our way and plunging ourselves into disaster.

The deliverance we need is from three main sources: the World, the Flesh and the Devil.

THE WORLD

As we have already seen, 'the whole world is under the control of the evil one' (1 John 5:19). There is corruption all around us and it threatens to invade our lives, drawing us little by little into sinful practices. We are pressurised from all sides to conform to what is acceptable in the eyes of the world.

To the Israelites, God said,

> You must not live according to the customs of the nations ... you are to be holy to me because I, the LORD, am holy, and I have set you apart from the nations to be my own (Lev. 20:23,26).

The Lord offered His people the highest standard of life but they refused to accept it. Instead of being holy and set apart for God, the people allowed themselves to be lured away from Him by the nations around them. They settled for a lower standard — the world's:

> you have not followed my decrees or kept my laws but have conformed to the standards of the nations around you (Ezek. 11:12).

Israel, the Old Testament chosen people, let God down. The Church is God's New Testament 'chosen people, a royal priesthood, a holy nation, a people belonging to God' (1 Pet. 2:9).

> Read the rest of 1 Peter 2:9 and consider the function of every believer.

As God's children we are meant to live in the light and not be drawn away by the standards around us into various degrees of shadow. The exhortation to us is fundamentally the same as it was to the Israelite nation, namely:

> Do not conform any longer to the pattern of this world, but be transformed by the renewing of your mind (Rom. 12:2).

We are different from non-Christians and our whole way of thinking should reflect this. Our minds need renewing from considering things in worldly ways. The world's standards are not God's, so they can't be ours either. When the world says that to get anywhere in life we must be educated, sophisticated, rich, married and well-known, there is a significant conflict with Jesus' assessment of success in Matthew 5:3–12:

> Blessed are the poor in spirit, for theirs is the kingdom of heaven.
> Blessed are those who mourn, for they will be comforted.
> Blessed are the meek, for they will inherit the earth.
> Blessed are those who hunger and thirst for righteousness, for they will be filled.
> Blessed are the merciful, for they will be shown mercy.
> Blessed are the pure in heart, for they will see God.
> Blessed are the peacemakers, for they will be called sons of God.
> Blessed are those who are persecuted because of righteousness, for theirs is the kingdom of heaven.

> Read these Beatitudes with a receptive heart, pausing after each one and praying it into your life. Don't be pressurised by time.

In Jesus' time everyone knew how religious and unworldly the Pharisees were. They gave to the poor, prayed and fasted but, as Jesus pointed out,

> Everything they do is done for men to see (Matt. 23:5).

Look up Matthew 23:27,28.

Consider how people today cover up the truth of what they're like by focusing on externals.

Pray that God will show you if you're guilty of this and give you discernment so that you can detect the real motives in people's hearts.

Pray that your motives and actions will be in harmony.

They claimed to be free but weren't because, like sheep, they all followed each other. When Jesus asked them whether John's baptism was from heaven or from men, they couldn't answer. If they had said 'from heaven' they would have had to explain why they hadn't been baptised. If they had said 'from men' they would have had to face the angry response of the people who held that John was a prophet. So they 'sat on the fence' and replied, 'We don't know' (Luke 20:7).

Compromise isn't only allowing the world's standards to invade our lifestyle, it can also be a 'sitting on the fence' experience. We don't actually identify with God's standards but we don't quite deny them either. Instead, we lapse into compromise. We simply fail to stand against 'shady things' we find ourselves doing, and by our acceptance of them we lower our standards and muddle in with the world. Beware. It has been well said that 'he who sits upon the modern fence is liable to be electrocuted!'

Read Galatians 1:10 and ask yourself the two questions there.

In what ways might you be compromising with the world?

The Flesh

We know that God 'richly provides us with everything for our enjoyment' (1 Tim. 6:17) but there is a point at which enjoyment of the things around us becomes over-indulgence. Jesus warned us to 'seek first his kingdom' (Matt. 6:33). This involves an act of the will which is followed up by positive action in a 'righteous' direction. If we turn away and begin seeking other things first, we shall steadily and subtly find ourselves being ruled and driven by our feelings and desires. King David, of whom God said:

> I have found David son of Jesse a man after my own heart (Acts 13:22).

fell tragically into adultery. If this happened to someone who pleased God as much as David did, surely none of us is immune from sexual or any other form of temptation.

> if you think you are standing firm, be careful that you don't fall! (1 Cor. 10:12)

The way to discover whether we're being controlled by our flesh is to examine the way we live. If we are over-indulging in one area (or more) we shall need to bring it to God and seek to re-establish His rule over it. For example, if we're becoming lazy and undisciplined, God will want to work with us to get us self-motivated again. This will probably mean that we shall have to stop allowing sleep and television to occupy our time. Something constructive will need to take their place. Now what the 'constructive alternative' will be will depend very much on us as individuals and our circumstances. God knows each of us intimately and has in mind how He wants us to use our time for His glory. If we're open to Him, He will make the way clear to us.

Consider the following problems: laziness/ indiscipline, overworking, preoccupation with appearance, pleasure-seeking, desire to possess, sexual desire, covetousness, habits (overeating, smoking).

Go through the list and work out what could be done to overcome each problem. For example: Problem: laziness/indiscipline. Possible remedy: avoid too much sleep/television, look for new daily goals, change diet, get more exercise.

Is God challenging you about any of these or about any other issues? What action do you propose to take?

Someone once said, 'Resisting temptation is usually just a matter of putting it off until nobody is looking!' Many Christians take this attitude and continue, often in secret, to allow themselves to be mastered by the flesh. The apostle Paul declared:

> All things are lawful for me, but not all things are helpful (1 Cor. 6:12 RSV).

He knew how strong the desires of his flesh were and he battled to keep his body under his control. If Paul had to fight to maintain self-discipline, how much more should we? Overcoming temptation doesn't just come naturally. We have to work at making 'no provision for the flesh' (Rom. 13:14 NASB) and we need each day to call upon God for help to deliver us from its cravings.

THE DEVIL

Paul exhorts us:

> Put on the full armour of God so that you can
> take your stand against the devil's schemes
> (Eph. 6:11).

We have a cunning enemy whose supreme objective is to keep everyone in the world as far away from God as he can. He works hard at preoccupying the unbeliever with as many worldly distractions as possible and he doesn't give up the attack when he sees individuals who are genuinely trying to walk with the Lord. It was in a perfect world that a perfect pair fell into the devil's hands (Gen. 3:6). Satan entered into Judas, one of the twelve disciples (John 13:27) and Ananias and Sapphira were lured away in the midst of a revival (Acts 5:1–11). If these people, and Jesus too, were approached by Satan, we should be foolish not to expect him to be interested in us.

Just as an effective enemy will keep his plan of campaign secret from the opposing forces, so Satan will not let us look over his shoulder at exactly how he proposes to upset our lives. He is clever enough to vary his tactics and tailors them to suit the vulnerability of each Christian. Truly he is as wise as a serpent! We can only defeat him in the strength and with the spiritual discernment which God supplies.

THE DEVIL'S SCHEMES

There is a subtlety in convincing argument. At times, the devil comes to us as an 'angel of light' (2 Cor. 11:14) and, by reasoning with us, attempts to draw us away from God's desires. Satan frequently (although not always) uses people who are close to us to do this. He knows how much we long to please those we love and capitalises on it. Peter, one of the three disciples closest to Jesus, rebuked Him for speaking of His death and resurrection. But Satan was behind Peter's words and Jesus recognised it (Matt. 16:23).

There's a subtlety in surprise. As a 'roaring lion' (1 Pet. 5:8,9), the devil has the ability to pounce on us — often when we least expect it. On these occasions he claws at our faith in God in a ferocious attempt to reduce us to a blubbering heap. It was Satan who was permitted by God to attack Job's family, his livelihood and his health (Job 1:13—2:10).

Let's not be naive in thinking that the devil has to approach us either as an angel of light or as a roaring lion. He is probably most successful when he combines the two — plausible suggestions with the occasional personal trauma thrown in. It is no wonder that we are exhorted to 'be alert' (Eph. 6:18). Soldiers who doze on the battlefield are asking for trouble!

THE DEVIL'S CLUTCHES

The devil seeks to lead Christians into spiritual darkness. His most obvious temptations have to do with occult practices — playing with ouija boards and tarot cards or reading horoscopes (even for fun). Most believers have renounced such things and refuse to dabble in them, but some find themselves led astray in other ways.

Jesus warned His followers to 'watch out for false prophets' (Matt. 7:15) many of whom would 'perform signs and miracles' (Mark 13:22) and deceive not just a few but 'many people' (Matt. 24:11). Peter underlined Jesus' words when he cautioned the believers to be on their guard against 'destructive heresies' (2 Pet. 2:1). John's first letter was actually written to encourage Christians to stand firm in the truth at a time when many were becoming sidetracked by false doctrines (1 John 2:26).

The Bible says:

in later times some will abandon the faith and

follow deceiving spirits and things taught by
demons (1 Tim. 4:1).

Satan is cunning. His schemes are lethal and we desperately
need all the wisdom and discernment we can get to maintain our
close walk with God. Peter exhorts us:

be on your guard so that you may not be carried
away by the error of lawless men and fall from
your secure position (2 Pet. 3:17).

He was speaking not to unbelievers but to believers. If they
could fall, so can we. We can drift off into error by becoming
preoccupied with particular doctrines and getting ourselves trapped
in little groups which hold to these. We can also become ensnared
by certain personal hang-ups which grip our lives and which we
may not recognise as problems because we have got used to them.
For example, we can become completely engrossed in the neces-
sity of health foods or bound up by certain negative beliefs about
ourselves which drive us to do certain things.

**Consider whether you might be controlled by a
particular doctrine, habit or belief. Seek God about
this.**

James promises us that if we submit to God and resist the devil
he will flee from us (James 4:7). In this part of the Lord's Prayer
we are submitting ourselves to God and praying that He will cause
us to recognise and avoid the devil's schemes. When we can see,
we can resist. The devil has no choice then but to leave us.

In conclusion, it's worth remembering that not only can all
Christians expect to be tempted, but they can also expect to be
delivered. The Word tells us that we will never face any temptation
which is too great for us to bear. There will always be sufficient
grace given to us to escape (1 Cor. 10:13). Jesus' victory over
temptation is available to everyone — let's enter into it.

To pray: And Lead us not into Temptation but Deliver us from the Evil One

Pray for deliverance today from the temptation to conform to worldly standards, to allow your flesh to control your desires and to be sidetracked by the devil into unhelpful actions/discussions.

Chapter Nine

FOR YOURS IS THE KINGDOM AND THE POWER AND THE GLORY FOR EVER

Some early manuscripts conclude the Lord's Prayer with the words 'For yours is the kingdom and the power and the glory for ever … Amen'. Other manuscripts do not. It is probably better for us not to close our time of prayer with the request to be delivered from evil but to reassure ourselves that God reigns supreme over everything. The Kingdom, the power and the glory are not ours, nor are they Satan's, they belong to God alone. Let us affirm this in our hearts — whatever our personal circumstances — as we go out into a new day.

> Praise be to you, O LORD,
> God of our father Israel,
> from everlasting to everlasting.
> Yours, O LORD, is the greatness
> and the power and the glory
> and the majesty and the splendour
> for everything in heaven and earth is yours.
> Yours, O LORD, is the kingdom;
> you are exalted as head over all.
> Wealth and honour come from you;
> you are the ruler of all things.
> In your hands are strength and power
> to exalt and give strength to all.
> Now, our God, we give you thanks,
> and praise your glorious name
> (1 Chron. 29:10–13).

**To pray: For yours is the Kingdom and the Power
and the Glory for Ever ... Amen**

**Remind yourself that God reigns over everything.
Begin the new day with boldness and expectancy —
you are the son or daughter of the King!**

Guide for Praying through the Lord's Prayer

Our Father in Heaven
Forget the problems which are concerning you at the moment. Relax with God — as His child. Talk to Him freely and naturally about things He has done for you recently, and thank Him for them.

For your notes

Hallowed be Your Name

Choose a hymn or worship song and sing it to the Lord. Ask God to bring to your mind one of His names.

Pause to allow Him to remind you of people/countries/circumstances, etc. into which He would like you to pray this name. Pray, trusting God to honour His name in each situation.

FOR YOUR NOTES

GUIDE FOR PRAYING THROUGH THE LORD'S PRAYER

Your Kingdom Come
Ask God to advance His Kingdom in: (choose from the following)

Jerusalem: your family situation
home — you and your family
church — holiness, power, evangelism, etc.

Judea: your involvement situation — school, college, workplace, club, neighbourhood, etc.

Samaria: a known situation —friends needing help/power, etc. A young people's conference, etc.

The ends of the earth: a world situation — a particular country/somewhere where there's been a catastrophe.

FOR YOUR NOTES

Your Will be done on Earth as it is in Heaven

Take time to reflect on and pray about the overall direction of your life. Pinpoint and pray through various issues in which you are seeking God's will to be done.

Pray that God will reveal any areas where you are resisting His will. Act on what He says.

FOR YOUR NOTES

Give us Today our Daily Bread

Put aside any false beliefs that God does not want to give good things to you.

Ask Him to provide for your physical needs (food, health, warmth, strength, finance), emotional needs (peace of mind, joy, security in God's love) and spiritual needs (closer walk with God, greater sensitivity to the Spirit, help in counselling).

FOR YOUR NOTES

Forgive us our Debts as we also have Forgiven our Debtors

Ask the Holy Spirit to reveal to you anything about you which may have offended the Father.

Ask God to forgive you and receive that forgiveness.

Ask the Holy Spirit to reveal to you if you are holding anything against any brother or sister. Forgive anyone who comes to mind. If necessary, put right by action the wrong you have committed — today.

FOR YOUR NOTES

And Lead us not into Temptation but Deliver us from the Evil One

Pray for deliverance today from the temptation to conform to worldly standards, to allow your flesh to control your desires and to be sidetracked by the devil into unhelpful actions/discussions.

FOR YOUR NOTES

For Yours is the Kingdom and the Power and the Glory for Ever ... Amen

Remind yourself that God reigns over everything. Begin the new day with boldness and expectancy — you are the son or daughter of the King!

FOR YOUR NOTES